Sugar:
My Journey Home

This book is a work of fiction. Names, characters, places, and incidents are either products of the author's imagination or are used fictitiously. Any resemblance to actual events or persons, living or dead, is entirely coincidental.

Copyright ©2015 by Heather Hamel

All rights reserved. No part of this publication may be reproduced except for brief extracts for the purpose of review with the express written permission of the copyright owner.

Cover art:
Editing by Pauline Malley
ISBN: 978-1514788080

Other books by Heather Hamel:

Horse Books:

Kobi: Memoirs of a Mustang
Sugar: My Journey Home
Saltos (Spring 2016 release)
Lefty (Spring 2016 release)

Ghostly Mysteries:

Murder of Crows
Destruction of Wild Cats (Fall 2015 release)

Cryptozoology Series

Within Emerald Forests (Book 1)
Under Sapphire Skies (Book 2)
Beneath Diamond Waters (Book 3) Fall 2015 release
Across Ruby Fields (Book 4) January 2016 release

Contact Heather at: heather.hamel@hotmail.com or through her website, www.HeatherHamel.com

For all the horses who are still looking for their forever homes!

CHAPTER 1 – MY RESCUE

A familiar rumble came down the road. I tried to place it, but my stomach rumbled as loud as the truck. The engine shut down in the front yard. My dirt pasture was out back. The brick two-story house blocked my view and rarely did visitors come to the rear of the house to see me. Still, the truck sounded familiar.

The front screen door slammed shut. Scott, my current human, must have gone out to see who arrived. I called him current because I've had so many humans throughout the years. A woman's voice reached my ears. The voice was as familiar as the truck.

Is Scott's wife back? Has Kate brought her horse, Patches, home, too? I hope so!

I was so lonely by myself. And hungry. Scott did the best he could, but hay twice a day just wasn't enough for me. My stomach rumbled again.

No. It's not Kate's voice. But it's still familiar.

My brain spun thinking back to all the women who had walked in and out of my life: Rosemary, Vickie, Kate.

Rosemary? Is that you? I'm back here. "Help! Get me out of here! I'm hungry!" I whinnied, hoping she'd hear me.

Her voice travelled closer. Did she hear me? She came through the side gate.

Rosemary! I was never happier to see someone. As always, her jeans were tucked into the tops of her worn cowboy boots, and she wore a sleeveless collared shirt. Her auburn ponytail poked from the back of her baseball hat. Rosemary's silhouette aptly indicated she was all horse inside. And her cap added to the evidence. On the front was a picture of a horse sailing over a jump. You know, I could never understand why a horse would do that when they could simply go around.

"Yup," she said to Scott. "That's the Sugar I remember." She never took her eyes off me. "She's a lot thinner than I remember, though."

Because I'm so hungry.

She turned to Scott. "I'll tell you what. Donate her to the rescue and I'll take her there myself. We need to put some work and money into her to get her back to where she needs to be."

Please, Scott. Donate me. Let Rosemary rescue me. I know she'll take good care of me. I know she'll feed me!

Scott didn't hesitate. "She's yours. Her registration's on the table."

Rosemary scratched my cheek before she followed Scott into the house. A few minutes later, her truck rumbled to life again.

"No! Don't leave," I whinnied. "What about the rescue place? Scott promised."

I didn't need to have worried. Rosemary walked around the corner, carrying a black rope halter.

You're back! Take me out of here.

She slid the rope up over my nose and flipped the top piece over my head. "Easy, girl. You're coming home with me."

I love you, Rosemary. And I truly did.

A hay net hung at the front of the trailer, filled to the top with fresh hay. I walked right in without a second look back at Scott. I grabbed a huge chunk of hay and tugged it out of the net.

Take me home.

*****

I backed out of the horse trailer, but it wasn't Rosemary's place. At her house, I had a smallish pasture that surrounded her house, and there were two other horses, Sunshine and Lulu. The three of us got along great — as great as three mares can — which meant we got along until someone was left behind, or someone grazed on another's favorite patch of grass, or someone received more attention from the humans than the other. Life with mares was so often filled with drama.

It was the rescue place. An abundance of smells assaulted my senses, too many to correctly guess the number of horses that lived there, but at least there weren't any dogs. I hoped some of the horses were geldings. They were easier to get along with. I looked around and saw grassy pastures dotted with horses. Small horses. Were they foals?

"Is this the mare you went to get?" a woman asked Rosemary.

"Yes, Candy. This is Sugar. I owned her a couple of years ago, and sold her to a friend who needed a big, level-headed horse. Came to find out that riding wasn't my friend's passion and so she sold Sugar." Rosemary handed my lead rope to the woman called Candy. "She'll be great for the kids. She'll stand for hours if you're grooming her."

"She's underweight and too tall for most of the kids. How much did you pay?"

Hey! I don't know you, but that's no reason to look at me as if you stepped in poop. If Rosemary thinks I'm a good horse that should be good enough.

"She was a freebie." Rosemary took my lead rope back. "Her owner fell on bad times. Got divorced, and as you can see, couldn't take care of her. She's a great horse. Or she used to be. We'll see how she is once she gets her weight up."

I'm still a great horse, Rosemary. I'll prove it to you.

Rosemary led me into a small stall. The size was more appropriate for tiny horses, not something my size.

"This will be your room for a couple of days, girl, until I make sure you're eating okay and figure out what pasture to put you in. If I remember correctly, you preferred geldings over mares."

Yes, I prefer to be where the boys are!

Rosemary scooped out some grain and poured it into a bucket.

Delicious! You've always had the best feed, Rosemary.

CHAPTER 2 – BOREDOM

It may not have been Rosemary's home, but she still spent almost every sunlit moment there. That didn't mean she gave me lots of her time though. Rosemary was in charge of so many horses, and nearly as many humans, that I only received fifteen minutes of her in the mornings. In that short amount of time she fed me, brushed my tangled mane, and picked my hooves.

On the first day, as soon as breakfast was over, she tossed me into a pasture with several of those small horses. They didn't even come up to my shoulder. Two were geldings and one was a mare. *Well, better than three mares.*

"Hi, I'm Sugar. Are you foals?"

"Ah, no," the mare said. I caught a hint of snobbishness in her voice. "I'm Sasha and we're all fully grown. We're just minis." Sasha was a cute, dapple grey with a full-length mane and a tail that dragged along the ground.

"Mini what?" I was genuinely confused. Were they a mini-horse, mini-pony? I've seen bigger dogs. Was she a mini-dog? She seemed like she could be mean enough to be a dog.

"A mini-horse, duh," the bay gelding said, his black forelock covering his eyes. "I'm Stefan and I can tell you aren't the smartest horse around."

"That's not nice," I snorted, hitting him with my tail. "I've just never seen anything less than a full grown horse that wasn't a foal."

Stefan puffed up at that comment. "We are not less than a full grown horse. We are fully grown. Fully grown for the type of horse we are. So watch yourself, girly. We were here first and we'll be here when you leave."

Stefan and Sasha wandered off to graze, leaving a little pinto behind.

"Well, unlike those two, *I'm* glad you're here. My name is Romeo and those two drive me crazy. Let's go graze in the shade and I'll let you know all about your new home."

We headed to some long grass near a group oak trees.

"Why are you guys so small?"

"We were bred to be this tiny. Typically people take us places that regular horses can't go. We meet people in hospitals and in nursing homes. We cheer them up."

"Like dogs? So you're—"

"Not dogs. We're horses. But yes, we perform the tasks that some dogs do."

"But you're big."

"Make up your mind. One minute you're insinuating we're too small, and the next—"

"I mean, compared to most dogs. I mean, I've seen some bigger dogs…." I was rambling now, but couldn't stop. I was shocked. I had known of service dogs and therapy dogs, but a *service horse*? Crazy!

"As we are horses, we are much better." Romeo sent me a wink. I could see how he got his name. He was quite charming.

"What do you guys do around here?" I asked.

"The minis stay quite busy. We travel to different places to meet city folk who may not know much about horses."

"You're put on show for them?"

"Yes, I suppose that's one way to describe it. We also work with children who can't ride. We pull them around in carts. It's fun and the kids seem to enjoy it."

"But I don't know how to pull a cart."

Romeo made a giggling sound. "Our carts are way too small for you. You may even be the biggest horse out here. Hmm, yes, perhaps. I'll have to think on that one. Anyway, the big horses are used for riding lessons to help people who fought in wars. They help heal their minds and spirits. It's called *wounded* something."

"Well, I might help, but I was hoping I'd be Rosemary's horse again." I swatted at a big fly that landed on my new friend's rump.

"Thanks. I don't think that'll happen though." He swatted a tail on the bottom of my belly.

I like him!

"Rosemary is in charge of the bigs and Candy is in charge of us minis. You may have met her when you came. This is her property and Rosemary just helps her run it."

I then understood why Candy had thought I was too big. She was in charge of the minis.

*****

I saw Rosemary every day. The minute the hunger pangs in my belly stopped, she put me to work in the round pen.

After putting me through my paces, she came up and rubbed my head. "I was afraid of this, girl."

Afraid? Afraid of what?

"Your stifle's gotten worse. With your legs I can't use you for lessons. Either you'll get hurt or someone will fall off during your unbalanced gaits. Candy's right, too. The kids and the Wounded Warriors are intimidated by your size, and that's just when you're in the pasture with the minis..." Her voice trailed off.

And? What does that mean?

"I've got to find you a home, girl, with people who will take you on trail rides, people who will take care of you, and your stifle."

Come on, Rosemary. We just started working together again. You'll think of something for me to do. You always do. You know how I hate being a pasture ornament. Please. We used to have the best adventures together. Remember?. Don't give up on me.

It was no use. I was turned back out with Stefan, Sasha and Romeo.

CHAPTER 3 – NEW BEGINNINGS

The open mouth of the horse trailer was welcoming, as if calling me to jump inside and head off on my next adventure. I was ready. It was time to go. Just as had happened many times before, Rosemary had started to treat me as a pasture ornament. There's so much more to life than just grazing in a field. I'm not a cow. I get bored too easily for that nonsense. Not to mention Stefan and Sasha made me crazy.

I never seemed to stay in any one place for too long, which was fine by me. And I hadn't yet found where I wanted to stay. Not yet. But I knew in my heart I was destined to be a great horse and do great things. I just had to figure out what it was and then convince whatever human I was with to join with me.

I swished my tail, smacking Rosemary with my long, black tresses.

"Sugar, you did that on purpose."

Yes, I did. Hurry up!

I could see clearly into the trailer. I liked that. There was nothing in there to worry me. I walked in and didn't look back, just as I had done when I left Scott.

The trip was short. Did I even make it off of the property? The trailer came to a stop and the truck fell silent. I heard voices. Male and female. They weren't familiar, but they sounded excited. That was typically a good sign.

My nostrils flared and I filled my lungs taking in as much air as I could, trying to learn a little about my new place. The grass smelled the same as the grass at my old place. But my nose picked out that there were many more flowering trees, which meant shade. I hoped some of the trees had pink flowers. Those were my favorite. I liked anything pink. There was also the distinct scent of one horse and the faded, lingering sent of another. One present and one gone. It was always that way. Some horses remained permanently and others moved from home to home. I was obviously the latter. I hoped one day to find a home interesting enough to want to stay. Maybe this was it.

The smells told me I'd have company. If there was one thing I hated, it was being alone. I backed out of the trailer and into a pasture flooded in sunlight. I inhaled again making sure I hadn't missed any scents the first time.

I smelled a dog. I hate dogs.

For some stupid reason, dogs found it exciting to chase me. I wasn't sure what would happen if I was ever caught, but I didn't intend to find out.

Gnats buzzed around my eyes and ears. I wasn't too crazy about that either.

Rosemary caught my lead rope and walked me to a new woman. The new woman smelled like lemon and of the other horse.

"Here ya go. Why don't you do the honors of leading Sugar to her new barn?"

New barn!

I always like the sound of anything after the word 'new': new rider, new horses to make friends with, new trail, new barn. Ah, new!

"Hey, Daisy," a man yelled. "Cuzzin's in the house and Kobi's in his stall, so if you want to bring the new girl in the backyard, it's safe now."

I was the *new girl*. So who was Cuzzin and who was Kobi?

"Thanks, Rex! We'll be back there in a minute," yelled the person holding the other end of my lead rope. Daisy? She must have been Daisy. And the man's name was Rex.

Daisy dropped her voice so only I could hear. "We're doing just fine right here, aren't we, girl?" She talked in fast, clipped words and stroked my neck just as quickly.

Hey, Daisy, what's the hurry? Slow down and enjoy life! Live slow!

It wasn't a bad-looking place. The fences dividing the pastures were in good shape. There was a sheltered, round bale of hay to snack on and just as my nose had guessed, lots of trees. And ones with pink flowers. One pasture had a small pond. I wasn't crazy about ponds. I could never see what might be in there. You could never tell what lurked beneath the water's surface. Anything could be waiting for a chance to leap out and attack some poor, innocent creature. Some poor, innocent creature like me.

Daisy tightened her grip on my lead rope and started walking. Fast. We were heading toward whatever awaited me in my *new* life. Ah, that word *new!*

When we turned the corner of a red, two-stall barn, the head of a dark horse peered over a wall. When I got closer, he nickered.

"Hello, there!" he said.

A gelding!

He was a small horse and seemed glad to see me. Life was always easier when I got along with my fellow horses. Daisy unclipped my lead rope. I wandered off and introduce myself. We touched muzzles, and I gently blew into his nostrils.

"Hi, I'm Sugar."

"I'm Kobi." He blew back and I thought he meant to be friendly. But then he pinned his ears and turned aggressive. "Just so you know, you're way too close to Daisy. Back off! She's *my* human and I don't share."

My initial assumption that he was nice was incorrect. Plus he was a gelding who was as sassy as a mare.

"You're a jerk!" I threw my head up and backed away.

"Kobi," said Daisy. "I'm not sure what you just told her, but you better be nice. She's part of our herd now." Daisy raised her arms and shushed Kobi back from the wall and deeper into his stall.

I turned my back on Kobi before dropping my head and grazing. I swished my tail, letting him know I meant what I said. He *was* a jerk.

Maybe I am destined to be Daisy's favorite horse. And if Daisy wants that, who can blame her? Who knows where life will take us?

"The horses will get things figured out." Rosemary tightened her ponytail. "It might take a few days for them to decide the new pecking order. Whenever we bring a new horse into the rescue, there's a lot of puffing and squealing at first. They'll quiet down. Don't worry about it."

"I just know Kobi." Daisy looked at the dark muzzle poking over the stall wall again. "He can be somewhat intense with new horses. I just hope he's not too mean to her."

"I wouldn't worry much about Sugar. She can hold her own." Rosemary scratched the black spot on my neck. I lifted my head and looked out over my new pasture. It was peaceful, no screaming kids. The pasture had a couple of ground poles and bright orange cones. *I wonder what they do up there.* I decided it was going to be a good place to call home for a while, even with the troublesome gnats.

"You mentioned Sugar has issues with her stifle." The lanky man called Rex walked out of the barn carrying a water bucket. "It won't keep her from running from Kobi if she needs to, will it?"

"Oh, no." Rosemary chuckled. "She'll know what she needs to do to take care of herself. She was one of the lead mares back at our place. Like I said, Sugar can hold her own."

I snorted. *You better believe it.* Kobi's black muzzle disappeared back into his stall.

Rosemary stopped scratching me, so I dropped my head and returned to grazing.

"It looks like she's settled in." Rosemary looked from me to Daisy. "Um, I hate to ask this, but can we get her halter back? We go through quite a few of them at the rescue."

"Absolutely. We have some extras lying around here. I'm sure one will fit her until we figure out her personality and can buy one to match."

Rosemary untied the halter by my cheek, and slipped the rope past my ears. "I know you'll enjoy her. She's a good girl. If you have any questions, let me know."

"I will, but as far as I can tell everything's good."

I'm better than good, and so far everything's great!

Daisy followed Rosemary out.

It was official. I was no longer Rosemary's horse. I was Daisy's horse now.

After Rosemary's truck and trailer rattled off the property and the front gate was securely latched, another female voice blended with Daisy's as she walked back to the barn.

Turning the corner, the other woman squealed. "Oh, a paint! She's gorgeous."

Now, I don't consider myself conceited, but I am pretty. I'm white, with large, shiny, dark-brown and black patches all over. My black tail floats along the ground when I walk, and I've heard more than once that my multi-colored mane is spectacular, if a bit on the short side.

"Ruth, meet Sugar," Daisy said.

I didn't lift my head, but kept an eye on her approach. She didn't touch me. She stood close, but off to the side. A grin stretched across her face as she circled around.

"I can't wait to ride her," Ruth said.

Daisy laughed. "Why don't you settle for just grooming her today?"

Kobi nickered over his stall wall. "Isn't it time to eat?"

"After dinner, of course," Daisy said to Ruth, smiling at Kobi.

I picked my head up at the mention of another of my favorite words. Dinner.

"I've got to get something out of my car," Ruth said. "I bought Sugar a *Welcome to the Barn* present."

"We'll wait for you right here," Daisy said. A few seconds ticked by. "I can't believe how bad the gnats are already." Daisy swatted the tiny, flying insects buzzing around her head. "I thought last year they didn't get bad until June. April is way too early for this."

"Do we have a fly mask that will fit her?" Rex asked.

"I'm not sure. Kobi's will be too small and Jake's will be too big."

There are two horses here? Where's the other one? Jake? Maybe he's nicer than Kobi. Why is one scent so much stronger?

"Hey, Rex, keep an eye on her, and I'll look in the tack room and see what we have that might fit her."

Rex stroked my neck while I grazed.

"It's okay, Sugar. Daisy and I are going to take good care of you. Don't pay any attention to Kobi. He's a bully at first, but after a while he'll back off."

I'm not worried. Like Rosemary said, I can take care of myself.

I picked my head up and nuzzled Rex. I liked him. He smelled like the dirt and trees, smells I trusted. He also spoke low and comforting words, and when he moved, he didn't make quick, sudden movements like Daisy. Maybe he would keep me for his own horse and we could do awesome things together like trail riding or western horse shows.

Daisy rushed back carrying a piece of green and gray mesh. I don't think she ever did anything without hurrying.

What is taking Ruth so long? I want my present. I hope it's something to eat. Or something pink. Or something new.

"This one should do the job." Daisy held up the mesh material. "It was Jake's, so it might be a little big."

I heard Kobi snort in his stall.

When Daisy got close to where I was grazing, she ripped the material open and level with my ears. She leaned over my head. She was going to put the material over my ears and eyes.

Oh, no. I backed out of range and threw my head into the air. *I'm not sure what that is, but it's not going on my head.*

"Do you think she's ever worn a fly mask?" Daisy asked, following me around the grassy pasture. At every turn I managed to stay just out of reach.

"Based on her reaction, I'd say no. I'm thinking we catch her and put a halter on her. It might make life a little easier on you."

"The only halter we have that would fit her is an old, rope one. She's going to have to stand still for a few seconds. I don't want to chase her all over the backyard."

"Tell you what, you get the halter and I'll catch Sugar. But I'll need you to tie it on her."

"Deal."

I studied Rex. Why did he need Daisy to tie the halter for him? I checked him out, starting with his feet. I liked his slow, calm methods much better than Daisy's *gotta get it done right now* attitude. My investigation of him stopped at the end of his arms. One hand was missing. *So that's why!* People needed two hands to tie things.

Rushing back to the barn, Daisy said, "I hope we haven't got ourselves in a bad situation with this mare."

"Remember what Rosemary told us," Rex said, walking up and stroking my neck. "We need to give Sugar a fair chance. So we have to keep her at least thirty days before we decide if we're giving her back."

Thirty days? And back where?

Daisy approached again, carrying something I recognized. A halter. I stood still while she tied the halter in place. When she finished, she handed the lead rope to Rex and marched back to the barn for the fly mask.

"I know you expect all our horses to know everything already," Rex said. "But why don't you try moving a little slower with her? Sugar's had some major changes in her life today and might be a little nervous around us."

Daisy sighed but didn't answer. Her shoulders relaxed and she brought her arms up much slower than the previous time. "It's okay, Sugar," she murmured, reaching to put the mask up and over my ears.

I tried to pretend I didn't mind her putting the mask over my ears and didn't toss my head around as much. I tried to pretend I didn't mind the mask coming down over my eyes. I realized I could see through it. I really didn't mind when she attached it under my throat. The gnats were instantly gone from my eyes. It wasn't as bad as I thought it would be after all.

Where is Ruth? Where's that present. I'm waiting!

"Since we're both standing out here, why don't you try taking it off and putting it on a few times?" Rex said.

"Good idea." Daisy reached for my throat.

R-R-R-RIP!

What was that? Something's biting my throat. I'm gonna die.

Whatever made that horrible noise didn't hurt. In fact, I didn't feel a thing, but I didn't want to take any chances. I threw my head up out of Daisy's reach, and backed up as fast as my legs would carry me. I didn't get too far. I forgot Rex was holding my lead rope.

"Oh no, missy. We're not playing this game." Daisy closed the gap.

I don't want to play this game either. You might be trying to kill me for all I know.

Daisy approached my head again. Rex kept a tight grip on the lead rope, not allowing me any escape, forcing me to stand still. Daisy manipulated the strap under my throat, closing it and then ripping it back open. The ripping seemed to grow louder each time I heard it, and each time the strap ripped, I threw my head up in the air and tried backing up. I never got too far. After what seemed like an eternity, I realized the sound wasn't going to hurt me and quit jumping and backing up. Satisfied I had accepted my fate and new mask, Daisy unclipped the lead rope.

"Let's give her some time to adjust before dinner."

Oh, no dinner yet? I love dinner. And breakfast, too.

Rex put his arm around Daisy and they headed into the house. I pouted just a little before dropping my nose down to graze again.

"A word of advice." Kobi poked his nose over his stall wall. "Don't let Daisy know you're afraid of anything. She feels it's her job to help you get over it, and sometimes she's a bit over the top about it."

I gave Kobi my back, letting him know I wasn't in the mood to forgive him for being so rude, not yet anyway. His nose disappeared back into his stall. I thought I heard him chuckle.

The new lady Ruth headed my way. She carried a white, plastic bag.

Do you have my present? What took you so long?

"You're going to love this." She pulled something bright-pink out of the bag. A halter. She bought me my very own pink halter, complete with a pink and teal, braided lead rope. Pink! I was in heaven.

Rex yelled, "Cuzzin, get back in here."

A dog barked.

"Cuzzin," Rex yelled again, then sent a high whistle through the air. "Inside!"

Heaven ... with a dog.

CHAPTER 4 – DAISY

I soon fell into the routine of my new barn. Each night Kobi and I were put in our stalls with a little grain and some hay. When the sun peaked above the horizon, Daisy came back out to the barn, gave us bran mash and more hay, put on our fly masks, and sprayed us for gnats and flying bugs. It was funny. I hated the fly mask but didn't mind the spray. Kobi was the complete opposite. He'd hang his head out of his stall for the fly mask to be put over his ears, but danced around as if the fly spray was made of acid as soon as it hit his skin.

    After breakfast, Rex let us out of our stalls. We were left to graze and run for much of the day, left pretty much alone to be horses, allowed to do whatever we wanted within the confines of the fences. I found one spectacular cypress sapling. It scratched my belly in all the right places as I walked over it. People sometimes met us along the far fence lines. They'd bring sweet treats. One man and his daughter gave us marshmallows. I didn't like the sponginess too much, but still ate them. Another man and woman brought apples. The big, red, juicy kind. Crunchy and delicious. If they were pink, they'd be perfect.

Every evening as the sun set, Kobi and I would be called back to the barn, given a grain mixture, and then released back out for a few more hours before being taken to our stalls for the night. All in all, it wasn't a bad routine. I was well-fed and bug-free, which was a greatly improved existence compared with some I had experienced. I especially liked the well-fed part. Sometimes the old dog Cuzzin would chase us around. The dog had this high-pitched bark that hurt his throat, or at least I was sure it did, and his tail wagged low to the ground. Kobi seemed to enjoy the sport. I didn't. Kobi would spin and Cuzzin would retreat. And then the chase started again. The dog had hip pain and couldn't run too fast, so rarely came close enough to do any damage. He was probably a good working dog in his youth.

Something was missing though. I was ready for some action. Preferably action that didn't involve my pasture mate. His kind of action, I did not want. If I didn't know better, I'd think snow clung to Kobi when he returned from his workouts. He was covered with white, foamy sweat. Yuck! While I wouldn't mind being ridden every once in a while, I'd prefer something slower paced than what he did. Dressage was not for me. All of those extended gaits and flexing my neck, not my cup of tea. Getting out of these pastures occasionally would have suited me just fine.

To say Daisy loved Kobi or preferred him over everything else, both human and equine, would be an understatement. The sun in Daisy's world rose each morning and set each night with that mustang. And it was reciprocated. He was groomed more than I, worked more than I, and I think he was even fed more. He always needed more time to eat his meals and I don't think it was because he was a slow eater.

One night, after Kobi and I had finished our bedtime hay, he came down to the end of his stall, and faced me across the breezeway.

"You know Daisy is my human?"

"I think you've mentioned that before." I swished my tail to let him know I wasn't going to let him bully me.

"I'm serious. I am the only horse she rides. I am the only horse she's ever going to ride. Do you understand?" Kobi pinned his ears.

I didn't answer. I walked to the other end of my stall and swished my tail again. No more was said. Maybe Ruth would come out again soon and groom all of my itchy spots.

While she hadn't ridden me yet, maybe she would soon. Or even Rex. Would Rex ever ride me?

*****

Daisy headed to my stall with a saddle.

Finally! I was going to get to do something!

Kobi glared my way. My belly tightened. He would not be in a good mood tonight. Kobi made it quite clear how he felt about sharing his human, but I wanted to prove to Daisy I was the better horse. Kobi might know all of those fancy dressage moves, but I don't think I'd spook at nearly half the things he spooked at.

His eyes followed our every move. Maybe he wouldn't be so cranky if he thought I didn't want to do it, so I put on a show for him. While Daisy was tacking me up, I pinned my ears. When it came time for Daisy to tighten my cinch, I swatted her with my tail. The tactic only worked once. The second time I tried to hit Daisy, she grabbed my tail with one hand while tightening the cinch with her other hand.

When she tried to get me to take the bit in my mouth, I tossed my head in the air, as high as I could stretch, then backed away until my rump hit the back wall. Seemingly not intimidated by my antics, she matched me step for step until there was nowhere else for me to retreat. She kept her hands high until my neck tired and I had to lower my head into her waiting arms.

After Daisy tacked me up, she led me to the front field and clicked on a lunge line. I'll never understand why humans feel that practice is beneficial. I don't think it's natural for an animal of my size to run in tight, small circles. It bores us to tears if the truth be known.

Kobi was confined in the back pasture. He could still see everything, but he couldn't interfere. Good idea. He wasn't happy when we left and probably would have tried to run me all over the field, Daisy around or not.

Daisy asked me to walk clockwise for a few circles before she clicked to me. I came to know that the click was the universal command to speed up, but I wasn't ready yet. I pretended not to know what she was asking me to do. Feigning ignorance has worked well for me in the past. My humans figured if I didn't know what they wanted, it meant someone else failed in my training. But not Daisy, no. She became more insistent I trot and cracked a whip at my hindquarters.

Alright, alright. I obliged.

I sped up into a trot. Trotting or walking fast have never been my favorite activities. Pounding my hooves into the earth made my legs hurt. Most horses love to run. Not me. Let me meander without lines or rails and I'm a happy mare. That was one of the many reasons I preferred trail riding over arena work.

"Oh, my," Daisy said. "Rex, can you see this?" She looked over to where Rex was pulling weeds.

"See what? What's she doing?" Rex straightened up from the ground and brushed dirt off his shirt with his right hand.

"I think she's trotting. She looks like she has legs from four different horses, and doesn't know how to use any of them."

Hey! There's no reason to make fun of me. I told you I wasn't good at trotting. I can walk slowly all day long, anything faster – well, I'm a little out of shape. Oh, yeah, and there's a problem with my stifle. But you already knew about that.

Daisy made me trot a few more circles then brought me back down to a walk and then switched to counter-clockwise circles. I thought we were done. I didn't want to walk in circles anymore, and I certainly didn't want to trot. But Daisy was insistent. Each time I tried to come in to her to end our lunging session, Daisy hissed like an angry cat and flailed her arms around like those inflatable creatures humans like to put in their yards during the holidays. There was no stopping until Daisy was ready to stop.

Rex walked over carrying a stool. He moved so much slower than Daisy. I like him.

That stool must be light if he can do that with one hand.

"You ready to hop on?" he asked.

Hop on? Daisy's riding me? What?

"I guess so," Daisy answered, not sounding the least bit confident. "I'm just going to walk her, though. I'm not sure if I can sit her trot. I'd hate to end our first session on the ground."

Kobi was standing at the fence. If Daisy hopped up and rode me, there would be a price to pay when I got back to the barn. But I guess it wouldn't do to pamper to Kobi's demands all the time. Jerk! I hated that he put me in such an awkward position, choosing between my human and my pasture mate.

Daisy stepped up on the stool. "Okay, Sugar. Here's your test. You have to be a good girl now."

When have I not been good? Oh, yeah, at the barn.

Rex was at my head, holding onto my bridle to keep me from moving off before Daisy was ready. *Like I'd do something like that. Well, okay, I've done it before. But only with Rosemary. And her husband. And that one time they used me during a little kid's birthday party. Okay, maybe holding my head isn't such a bad idea.*

Daisy put her foot in the stirrup and swung up into the saddle. Rex let go of my bridle and stepped away.

Okay, now what? I waited for Daisy's first command.

"Walk," Daisy said, gently squeezing my sides.

I took a few tentative steps forward and stopped. Daisy was nervous. I felt her tension run down her legs through the saddle. I don't think she wanted to be up there anymore than Kobi wanted her there.

"Walk," Daisy said again, squeezing me a little more.

We started walking around the front field, under Rex and Kobi's watchful eyes.

"How's she doing?" Rex asked.

"She feels fine. A little slow, but I'm good with it. I'd much rather have a slow horse than a hot horse. I'm just always nervous riding on a new one. Kobi has me spoiled."

As if on cue, Kobi screamed across the pasture, "No! Get down!"

Daisy tightened her hold on my reins, cuing me to stop. I did. We waited until Kobi's temper tantrum passed, then started walking again. Kobi threw another scream to the air. Daisy tightened up on the reins yet again.

No need to choke me. I tossed my head to take some of the reins from her hands.

Kobi screamed a third time. I stopped walking. Daisy sighed.

"I'm going to hop down. She hasn't done anything stupid yet."

And I'm not going to. Give me a chance. Kobi's the one screaming like a banshee and running around like an idiot. Not me.

"With Kobi having a fit, I don't want Sugar to spin to see what he's yelling about."

"Why do you think he's acting all weird?" Rex asked.

"Because I'm up here. He was just fine the entire time I was lunging her. He didn't start screaming until I climbed up. He's either afraid I'm going to take Sugar off the property and away from him …"

Not a chance!

"…or he doesn't want me riding her."

Now you've got it.

"Hold her while I dismount."

Rex came to hold my head. With Daisy off my back, Kobi returned to grazing, pretending to ignore us. I knew better. His ears followed our every move.

Back at the barn, Daisy slid the bridle off over my ears, and traded it for my new pink halter. Leaving me tied when she went into the tack room, I heard her unscrew the lid to the cookie jar.

Mmmm, cookies.

Kobi heard it too, and rushed over. As soon as Daisy walked from the tack room, the scent of apples and cinnamon hit my nostrils. I inhaled, pulling the smell deep into my nose.

I love those cookies.

Kobi nickered to Daisy, demanding his treat.

"Patience, Kobi. Sugar gets her cookie first. She worked, you didn't."

I took the treat from her hand with my lips. *Ah, my reward for a job well done.*

Daisy gave Kobi a treat as well before taking off my saddle even though he didn't do anything. *Must be nice to be her favorite.*

"You did pretty good today, Sugar. You're a little lazy and not a smooth ride, but you didn't try to dump me. I appreciate a solid horse. You didn't even get goofy when Kobi started screaming." Daisy turned her attention to Kobi. "You, on the other hand, were a dork. I'm not sure why you were mad, but screaming like a mad man is unacceptable behavior. I'll be riding Sugar and leaving you behind at times and no amount of tantrums will stop it."

Daisy swung the saddle and pad off my back.

As soon as she was out of ear shot, Kobi pinned his ears at me. "We'll just see about that."

CHAPTER 5 – MY STORY

Kobi's cold shoulder grew more and more maddening. It was dull without someone to talk to, someone to hang out with, someone to watch my back when I napped, someone to keep Cuzzin from chewing on my leg. I mean Daisy and Rex were there every day. Ruth came to visit once a week, and every couple of weeks Daisy's mom Holly would come to ride me. But in between those visits it was utterly boring.

Over hay that night, I asked, "What's your problem with me, Kobi?"

"I don't have problems. I just don't like you." He didn't bother looking up from his hay. He wasn't making this easy.

"Well, why don't you like me?"

"You're not Jake," Kobi said, as if that explanation was enough. "He's the one who belongs over in that stall, not you."

"Who's Jake?"

"Jake was my best friend. Rex was his human." A faraway look visited Kobi's eyes.

I wondered if it was Jake's lingering scent I caught on my first day. I waited for Kobi to explain more, but nothing came.

"You and I could be friends, too," I suggested.

"Not likely." Kobi's words were muffled by his mouthful of hay, but I understood him well enough.

Since it didn't look as if I would be leaving this new barn anytime soon, and it also appeared Kobi wasn't willing to accept my presence, I had to be the one to make it work. I had the same problem with Sasha when I first arrived at Rosemary's. She didn't want to be friends and made no bones about it. But I've never had an issue with a gelding – until now. Okay, and maybe once with Stefan, but I eventually won him over and the other horses there as well and I would here, too.

"So, what happened to Jake? Where is he?"

I waited for Kobi to answer. Just when I thought he wasn't going to, he coughed.

"He was sick. Something was wrong with his hoof. Daisy and Rex tried to help but they couldn't. They tried everything but nothing worked. Then he stopped walking and could barely stand."

Kobi shuffled around in his stall. His dark head popped over his wall and he stared out at the side pasture. I followed his gaze to a grassy place under a large tree. I had seen enough horses lay down and never get back up to know what happened to Jake.

"I'm sorry," I whispered. "I know it's never easy to lose a friend."

"No, it's not. I miss him every day." He paused. "So what's your story?"

I was caught off-guard. I didn't expect Kobi to reply, much less ask *me* a question. Were we finally going talk things out?

I thought about his question for a minute and finished a mouthful of hay. "What do you want to know?"

"The nights are long, so why don't you start at the beginning. And feel free to keep eating, Jake always talked with his mouth full."

"I don't remember much before meeting Rosemary the first time. She was looking for a horse big enough to carry a large rider, a rider who had no idea how to ride. After meeting me, Rosemary knew I would be the perfect horse for her friend Vickie. I was big, beautiful and laid back enough not to get worked up into a frenzy and throw anyone.

"I was the perfect trail horse. I've never been comfortable being a lead horse. Thankfully Vickie just wanted to follow the others on the trail. Aside from all of her weight on my back, it was almost the perfect situation. I learned to stand next to either a ladder or the back of a truck so she could climb up in the saddle. She was much too large to hoist herself up without some sort of help. My job on trails was to walk and make sure she stayed on my back.

"One day we were walking down a steep hill and Vickie, who was a bit top-heavy to start with, rolled out of the saddle, off my back and down the hill. I couldn't believe it. I had never had a rider just roll off my back like that. I didn't want to get blamed for something which was clearly her fault, so I wandered off into the trees and palmettos to graze. It was a fair distance away. Vickie couldn't see me, and I couldn't see her."

Kobi chuckled in his dark stall.

"But I could hear her. Vickie called and called for me. I decided I should help her find me, but by that time my reins had tangled on the palmetto bushes. Not only could I not go to her, but I couldn't even graze anymore. I was stuck. Stuck on an empty stomach. After what seemed like an eternity of just standing, Rosemary found us. She had retraced our steps and found me waiting in the bushes. Vickie decided she wasn't physically cut out for horseback riding and she sold me to an appaloosa ranch. Being a paint horse in an appaloosa barn, I stuck out like … well, a paint horse in an appaloosa barn. I was at least a hand taller than most of the others and where they had spots of different colored hair, I had patches. Out in the field, they all wanted to be my friend and grooming partner when the bugs were bad. They had the shortest tails while mine dragged along the ground. So when I swished it, I would take care of their bugs as well as my own. They made better friend choices than I did as I could keep the flies from them, but their little tails couldn't keep the gnats off me.

"One day another paint came to our pasture. Patches. He was such a handsome boy. He was also a tricolor paint but had much more black on his coat than I did. Being the only two paints in fields of appaloosas we became best friends, and left the appaloosas to fight off the bugs themselves.

"Patches hadn't been there long, when we were both sold to Kate. She had her eye on Patches and bought me as a gift for her husband Scott. I was turned into a trail horse for a large person without much horse sense again. She had much higher expectations for Patches. She rode him every day, conditioning and training him for competitions."

Kobi was listening intently to my story. I didn't want to audibly say my thoughts. His interest would surely lapse.

So instead I kept the words *kinda like Daisy does with you* inside my head.

"During those times, I stayed in the barn. I only came out to walk the trails with her husband Scott on my back. I didn't mind the trail rides, but I hated when they left me behind in the pasture. I remember those two humans yelled at each other and fought a lot. Since Kate confided in Patches during their rides, he knew much more than I did. Kate and Scott were ending their eight-year marriage and were getting divorced. And they were splitting us up, too. Patches stayed with Kate, and I stayed with Scott.

"With Scott, I was alone all the time. I don't think he meant to neglect me. He seemed nice enough. He just had no idea what he was doing or what he needed to do to keep me healthy. Without regular feeding times, pretty soon my grassy field turned to sand. He tossed me hay every day but it was nowhere near enough to keep me busy or full. The sandy ground chipped and cracked my hooves, but I guess it also helped keep them filed down somewhat since he never had a farrier come out.

"One day I heard a familiar truck, looked up from my hay flake and saw Rosemary. I was so happy to see her again and even happier when she loaded me into her trailer. I was going home. But she took me to a place that rescued horses, rehabilitated them, and gave them jobs. At first they wanted me to work with children, but my back is so high the children couldn't groom me, and were too afraid to ride me. I was sent out to pasture. I didn't like it. Dull and boring. Then I came here and I still feel as if I'm stuck in a pasture all the time and not given something fun to do, something to keep me busy. I want to work. A little anyway."

I fell silent. The sky was streaked with pink. My favorite color! I had talked all night. I was tired, but my story was told.

"You've been through a lot of humans. It's hard to believe you've had that much bad luck. You're not that old."

Was Kobi trying to tell me he didn't believe a word I said? I refused to think on it.

"By the way," I said, "earlier today I didn't plan for Daisy to ride me. I understand she's your human."

"I know," Kobi said. "It'll be fine. I think she's just getting you ready for Rex. She wants to make sure you'll be safe and sane for him. I just yelled to keep both of you on your toes, well, hooves for you."

"Oh, but she was so mad at you for doing that."

"I'm sure she was. But it worked. Now she'll think twice before leaving me alone when she rides you again. You'll see."

"Hey, why doesn't Cuzzin bite you? He's got it in for me for some reason."

"I kicked at him once when he got a little too close. Well twice actually. He was a slow learner."

After confiding in the little mustang, I realized how much I had been holding back and how much I needed a friend. After that night, our relationship changed. Kobi grew much more tolerant when I worked with Daisy. He gave me advice and helped me to understand my new home. Advice like when Daisy attempted to desensitize us to something, it was best to just give in. She'd eventually stop. And Rex wouldn't make me work for cookies like other people. It was best to be nice and hang out when he cleans the stall. Rex was great with treats. And most important of all the grass in the backyard was considered a horse-free zone, or as Kobi called it: the Forbidden Zone. Only on very special occasions, like when I first arrived, did any horse get to graze back there.

CHAPTER 6 – REX'S RIDE

Something was different the day Rex walked to the pasture with my pink halter slung over his shoulder. Daisy haltered Kobi. Her back seemed a little tighter and straighter than usual. My first thought was to move away from Rex and play a game, make him catch me. But something about the way Rex walked made me realize there wasn't much of a point. I lowered my head and placed my nose in my halter for him.

"Good girl," he told me, rubbing my ears. "We're going for a ride with Daisy and Kobi today."

Kobi had been right. Rex was going to ride me. Was I finally to have a job of my own? Finally be a trail horse?

It turned out Rex wasn't the strongest or most confident rider. I heard them talk about a time he'd been thrown, and Daisy was now a nervous wreck. She didn't want him to get hurt again. And missing his left hand, he would be expecting me to neck-rein and follow the pressure on my neck instead of steering me by direct contact with my bit.

Daisy and Ruth had been working on fine tuning my reining, but what if I wasn't ready? What if Rex expected more from me than what I could do? Rex finished brushing me and Daisy came over to pick my hooves. My nerves hit breaking point. I was dancing around my stall instead of standing still like usual. Why was I so jittery? I could look after Rex. I knew I could.

Daisy whispered in my ear, "I'm trusting you with Rex. Don't try anything stupid. Do you understand me?"

I heard Daisy loud and clear, but it didn't help my nervousness one bit. In fact, it made it worse.

Rex returned with my saddle. I didn't move a muscle as Daisy tightened my girth for him. She handed the reins back to Rex and he led me out of my stall and over to the mounting block. Daisy was already there, waiting, ready to hold my head to make sure I didn't walk off while Rex mounted. How did she do that? One second she was beside me, the next she was out by the mounting block. She didn't need to worry about me walking off while he mounted though. I wasn't even going to twitch a fly off my skin. Daisy let me know what I needed to do and I wasn't about to do anything to disappoint them. I was ready to prove myself.

Rex put his foot in the stirrup and swung up into the saddle. I was a little surprised when his weight dropped on my back. He was lighter than Vickie but heavier than Daisy. She fussed around us for a few more minutes, touching my neck and making adjustments to my reins and Rex's stirrups.

Rex and I were finally left alone. He squeezed me gently with his legs and commanded, "Walk."

I did. I took orders from his legs *and* his voice. We came to a tall pine tree in the pasture and I felt strong pressure on my right ribs and the reins touched my neck on the right side, making my mane move. I tried to think back to my training with Daisy and Ruth. What did that pressure mean again? While I was thinking, the pressure on my ribs increased, pushing me over to the left.

That's it!

I turned to the left, careful to avoid scraping Rex's knee on the bark.

"Good girl," Rex said, leaning over to scratch my mane. "I knew you were smart."

We circled and wove around trees neck-reining the entire time. It was easy, and Rex seemed pleased. That meant Daisy would be pleased. Rex and I were going to have a great ride together.

We headed back to the barn to pick up Kobi and Daisy. Kobi still wasn't fully tacked up yet.

"How'd she do?" Daisy asked while tightening Kobi's girth.

"Great," Rex answered. "It took her a minute to figure out neck-reining, but she's got it now. I can't seem to get situated in the saddle though."

Really? I thought you were fine.

Daisy peered over Kobi's back, looking at how Rex was perched. Then he did something I didn't expect. He bounced up and down in the saddle trying to find a more comfortable position.

My first thought was to scoot out from under Rex's bouncing. But before my feet would move, Daisy's words rang in my ears. My eyes grew wide, I held my breath but I stood my ground.

"Ah, there we go," Rex said, settling into the saddle. "I found the right spot."

"I'm glad you did," Daisy laughed, leading Kobi out of his stall. "I don't think Sugar could've taken too much more of your bouncing. Next time, move your legs around to find your seat, but keep your butt in contact with the saddle."

Thanks, Daisy.

Daisy swung up onto Kobi's saddle with ease. "And that's how you do it. Ready?"

We followed Kobi and Daisy out the gate and into the woods. I relaxed a little knowing Rex wouldn't be schooling me. If given a choice between working circles in the front field and weaving in and out of cones and ground poles, or taking a trail ride in the woods, I'd pick the woods every time. The sunlight filtering through the trees, the birds twittering, walking through nature; it was a much better way to spend the day.

I stepped gingerly through fallen branches. They were the type I really hated. Little branches curling like fingers and coming up out of the earth to claw my legs. Kobi was gaining ground getting further and further away. I did what I thought was the sensible thing and broke into a trot.

I was free from the grasping branches and made some gain on Kobi, when slaps hit my back and pressure pulled at my mouth. Rex! I felt him tense up, lose his seat and slide, just a little, but enough to worry me.

"Whoa, girl," Rex said.

I stopped. Rex settled himself back in the saddle, without bouncing this time. Kobi and Daisy stopped, too.

"What happened? Are you okay?" Daisy's words rushed like water overflowing its bank, even faster than she usually spoke.

"I'm fine. I think she stepped on some branches and panicked. She tried to trot her way to safety, but stopped after one or two steps."

Rex sounded calmer than he felt. I could tell. His seat was tense and his legs were stiff and he was holding my reins a little too tight.

I knew then why Daisy was so concerned about our ride. She knew Rex didn't have a great deal of confidence or a secure seat. He didn't have the control two hands allowed. He could only use his right one. That day was a test for both of us, to see if he was ready to ride again and if we'd be a good match. I wanted both of us to pass the test.

Had I just failed? Would Daisy consider my trotting inappropriate behavior?

Kobi's expression didn't offer any clues. He always wore a half-interested, half-bored look while standing still. I vowed then and there to be more cautious and a little safer when I had Rex on my back. Rex needed me to take care of him and I needed him if I was to get out of the pasture.

CHAPTER 7 – CLICKER TRAINING

Ruth and Daisy headed out to the barn after dinner one evening. Daisy wore a particularly serious look.

Kobi groaned. "Every time Daisy is that intense about something, she wants to try something new. This can't be good."

New? I loved that word. My ears perked up.

Ruth was doing all the talking. Daisy was doing all the listening. They grabbed our halters off the hooks by the door and came into our stalls. Ruth came to me and Daisy went into Kobi's stall, just as they usually did.

Their one-way conversation continued, with Daisy starting to introduce some nods and some *oohs* and *ahs*. I wasn't crazy about what was happening. I'd become used to Ruth talking to me and telling me about her day. When she did, she'd groomed me better, paying close attention to all of my white patches. When she was distracted, her brush strokes were a little harsh, almost painful to my sensitive skin, and my legs were hardly touched and remained crusted with dried mud.

When I heard Kobi snicker, I knew whatever the women were scheming about didn't involve him. He seemed to think it was hysterical when it was my hide on the line and not his. I had to focus less on my ungroomed and over-groomed spots, and more on what they were saying.

Daisy sprayed fly spray on Kobi and said to Ruth, "So just to make sure I have everything straight, you're trusting Sugar and her ability to learn to bow to help you with your grades in Behavior Modification? What if she can't do it?"

Bow? What is a bow? I had never heard of that before.

"She will." Ruth scratched my ear. "The only thing you'll need to do is video tape us before the last week of my class so I can turn it in as proof."

"Well, you seem confident, I suppose. So, alright." Daisy spoke slowly. Strange for her. And it was said in a tone that intimated she was more than skeptical about me learning whatever it was Ruth needed me to learn.

I can do anything. I'll show you. I'll do the best bow ever. As soon as I figure out what it is.

Ruth slid my halter off my ears. "Let's do this."

I'm about to figure it out, I think.

She stood at my shoulder. I knew she had some cookies. I could smell the apple cinnamon goodness. I swung my head around toward my haunches, figuring she wanted me to bend and work on my flexibility like Daisy was always trying to get me do. No. No cookie. I tried backing up. No to that, too. I had no idea what Ruth wanted me to do to earn my treat.

She tapped my shoulder, where my leg met my ribs.

What does THAT mean? I just stood there, waiting for another command. Ruth brought the cookie up to my nose, allowing me to fill my nostrils with the smell of apple and cinnamon.

Mmmm. I licked the roof of my mouth then started smacking my lips. I could almost taste it. Before I could take it from her hand, she lowered the cookie to my chest. I followed the scent.

Click!

What was that? I jerked my head up, away from the sound.

A few long seconds passed and nothing bad happened. I looked to Ruth. *What was that noise?*

She offered me the cookie she'd been holding.

Mmmm. The tastes burst in my mouth. That's what I had been waiting for. *Can I have another?*

Another appeared in her hand. Ruth stayed by my shoulder, tapping the treat where my shoulder met my ribs, but this time it was a little more forward, closer to my chest.

I twisted my head around, trying to reach her hand. Stretching sideways was never one of my talents. My head wasn't even close to reaching Ruth or the treat. Ruth brought the treat to my nose where I could smell it again.

Again it was gone. Ruth slowly moved her hand down towards my chest. In an apple and cinnamon dreaming daze, I followed the scent. My nose touched my chest.

Click!

Before I could jerk my head out of the way, Ruth offered me another cookie.

The second its flavor was off my tongue, my brain started racing. *When I touch my chest, something makes a loud click. And after I hear that sound, I get a treat.*

I got it! Ruth doesn't want me to bend or back up. She wants me to touch my chest. Why didn't she say something? I can do that.

Testing my theory, I bobbed my nose to my chest. No treat. I sighed. I thought I had figured it out.

Ruth started laughing. "I'm glad you've caught on, Sugar, but you have to wait until I ask for it. I can't have you going around bowing every time you want a cookie."

"That would be hysterical," Daisy said. "Especially if she could walk and bow at the same time."

So I'm right. I think I'm figuring out this bow thing.

Daisy wandered over to Kobi and gave him some attention.

Ruth touched that spot again, where my shoulder met my ribs. Still thinking I had the game figured out, I touched my nose to my chest.

Click!

I lifted my head and swung towards Ruth. She rewarded me with a cookie.

I knew it. Okay. When Ruth touches my shoulder, I touch my chest. Piece of cake. Or more accurately, piece of cookie. And that's a bow?

I waited for Ruth to ask me first, then I touched my chest a few more times to get a few more cookies. I liked the new game.

*****

Ruth came back the next day to play our new game again. She touched my shoulder and I touched my chest to get a click and a cookie. Then she moved her touch further down between my front legs. I touched the spot I had come to learn would get a click and a cookie. Nothing. Ruth must have changed the rules, but didn't tell me what they were.

What do you want me to do now?

I kept touching my nose to my chest, but didn't get a click or a cookie. Frustrated, I hit her fingers with my nose.

Click!

She handed me a cookie.

I did it? I need to touch your fingers now?

We did it a few more times before Ruth's hand sunk a little farther. Instead of my chest, she touched the inside of my front leg, a little above my knee.

I had to think about how to do this one. I knew my neck wouldn't bend the correct way in order to touch her fingers from where I stood.

Her tapping became more insistent. "Bow," she said.

Bow? That's easy. I touched my chest like I had the previous day.

"No." She laughed. "That wasn't a bow. You need to put your leg out first."

I do?

She kept tapping above my knee. She said I needed to move my leg out. That would make bending my neck a little easier. I moved my leg forward and touched my nose to her fingers.

Click!

"You did it!" Ruth was so excited she squealed. She gave me the cookie and threw her arms around my neck. She had me bow a few more times before she yelled across the pasture to where Daisy was riding Kobi. "She did it!"

So there!

Daisy smiled, and then suddenly her face fell serious. "Cuzzin!"

Cuzzin barked, and barked again. And then again. He was getting closer. He was heading straight for me.

"Cuzzin, no!" yelled Daisy.

"Cuzzin, no!" yelled Ruth.

Cuzzin, no!

But it seemed Cuzzin didn't understand the word 'no'. He didn't even slow as he flew under the fence. There was no sign of his gimpy hip. The old dog was set on causing trouble. He barked twice. I shifted back. Cuzzin stopped not six feet in front of me. He crouched. I shifted back again, then he scampered around to my side keeping a little distance.

"Cuzzin!" Daisy yelled angrily.

I shifted again. I needed to keep an eye on the dog. He seemed reluctant to attack when he knew I could see him. Before I knew it Cuzzin was behind me, and I felt a nip at my hind leg.

"Kick!" yelled Kobi.

And I did.

I guess Cuzzin performed some acrobatic twist in the air, because I heard him land near the fence.

Daisy was off Kobi and yelling at Cuzzin to get inside. The dog headed off quite sheepishly.

"Nice work," said Kobi.

"And it only took me one kick," I replied.

CHAPTER 8 – TRUST

As spring led into summer, I became the horse Daisy turned to when friends wanted to ride. Was it because she considered Kobi as *her horse*, or because I was solid and reliable and didn't try to bite or pretend to spook like a certain mustang when someone other than Daisy jumped on his back? Either way, it was nice to have a job.

One morning when Daisy's mother Holly was in town, Rex had a visitor of his own; his young granddaughter Clementine. Typically when Holly visited, my job was to take her trail riding alongside Daisy and Kobi. And when Clementine visited, Daisy would strap a tiny kids' saddle on my back, plop Clementine on top, and Rex would lead me around.

But this day, both Holly *and* Clementine were walking my way. I was curious how things were going to work.

Daisy headed for Kobi with halter in hand. Holly slid my halter over my ears, then handed my lead rope to Clementine to lead me back to the barn.

What? Clementine barely comes to my shoulder. What is she doing leading me? Um, Daisy? Are you seeing this?

Holly walked beside Clementine and took hold of my lead rope in time to walk me into my stall and tie me up. Daisy had already tied up Kobi. Her lips were squished together and I could see the muscle in her jaw flexing.

Say something!

She didn't.

Daisy, say something!

Still nothing.

Holly explained to Clementine the purpose of each brush and how to use it. Then she handed the brush over, and moved away from me. I didn't move a muscle or even swish my tail. I didn't want to risk hurting the little girl. I held my breath when she moved behind me. She brushed in fine, light strokes as far as she could reach. I was glad Holly finished the top of my back and hindquarters. I always like my white patches to glisten.

Holly returned from the tack room with the big, black saddle she always used. I released the breath I'd been holding.

I was so glad it was Holly who was going to ride. That meant a relaxing trail ride and not a kid. Kids! They tended to talk too loud and forever asked whoever was leading me to go faster just so they could bounce against the saddle on my back.

Kobi was saddled, but standing alone in his stall. *Where's Daisy?* As soon as the thought crossed my mind, she walked past me carrying the mounting block and Clementine's helmet.

Now I'm really confused. Who's riding today?

Daisy helped Clementine put on her helmet. Holly led me out of my stall.

You're wearing a helmet, too? What's going on?

Clementine stepped up onto the mounting block and Daisy grabbed my reins. Her jaw was still set. She wasn't comfortable with what was going on. That made two of us.

Holly handed Clementine the riding crop she used to clear spider webs from our path on the trail. "Here. You can hold this for me."

Holly hoisted Clementine onto the front part of the saddle, before stepping onto the mounting block herself. *They're riding double?*

"Now, wait a minute," Daisy said.

Phew. Thank you. You agree this madness has to stop.

"You are not to touch Sugar with that crop, do you understand?" She asked Clementine. "Sugar's being a very good girl letting you both ride. The first time I see it coming anywhere near her skin, you lose the privilege of holding it. Got it?"

No!

"I won't." Clementine twirled the crop in her hand.

"It'll be fine." Holly swung into the saddle behind Clementine. "You worry too much."

Daisy didn't say another word, but I could hear her breathing. It was louder than usual. The riders settled on my back.

Daisy leaned close and whispered, "I'm sorry, I had no idea. Take care of them though." Then she did something I never thought Daisy would do. She kissed my cheek. Ruth had kissed me. Rosemary had kissed me. Steve and Kate always kissed me. Holly too. Clementine had kissed my ears a couple of times. Even Rex puckered up to my cheeks. But never Daisy.

How bad is this about to get?

Daisy stepped back. Holly squeezed with her legs cuing me to walk. I moved off slowly, in case Daisy wanted to call me back or Holly changed her mind.

Daisy, I'm all ears. Holly, isn't there something else you'd prefer to be doing today?

Nothing.

I felt Clementine wiggle around, but Holly didn't change her command. I kept walking. The tree beside me exploded with movement. I wanted to run back to the safety of the barn. I tucked my rump under me. My reins tightened.

"No," Holly said, steering me from the barn. More trees exploded and shook violently.

What is going on?

"Clementine!" Daisy yelled from the barn. "The next time you hit a tree with your crop, you lose the privilege to ride. Got it?"

That was Clementine making all that trouble? Why wait, Daisy? Take her down now!

"Give it to me," Holly said. She took the crop from Clementine and circled me around to the gate leading to the front field.

I felt someone sink down into the saddle.

"I know," Holly said to the bouncing, former whip-wielding little girl. "You know how crazy protective Daisy is. She doesn't want anyone to get hurt."

We circled trees. None of them exploded. We circled cones until Daisy and Kobi finally joined us.

"Ready to hit the woods?" Daisy asked.

Hit? Don't mention hitting please, Daisy. Not when there's a crop close to my head.

"Time to get down, Clementine," said Daisy.

Clementine fussed about not being able to ride with us, but Daisy insisted riding double on the trails wasn't safe.

Phew. I'm so glad she did.

For the most part, the rest of the ride was uneventful. Kobi walked in the lead and alerted on every little thing from a three-day-old deer track, to a faint smell without a solid location. He was the most nervous horse on a trail ride that I'd ever encountered. Sometimes Daisy had no choice but to dismount and lead Kobi through something imaginary, something I assumed he believed would kill us all.

"Let's do the full loop," Daisy said, turning around in her saddle. "It branches off up here."

Kobi and Daisy disappeared down the trail to the right.

I don't want to go down there. Palmettos surrounded both sides of the path. There's no telling what's in them. It's too dangerous. Oh no. Am I sounding like Kobi?

I felt pressure on my left side, pushing me to follow. *Oh well, if he's going, I'm going!*

We weren't down the trail very far when something to our left rustled in the palmettos. It was a little ahead of me, but directly beside Kobi.

It rose its enormous black body out of the thick underbrush and outspread its massive wings. Up it went into the air. The beast was as large as Kobi's body. Kobi spun but got caught up in the palmettos.

I turned cleanly and took off at a bouncy, uncoordinated trot. I didn't see the need to canter. If the bird came back, Kobi was stuck in the bushes, and surely it would take time to kill the stuck horse and the rider, before the bird set its sights on me.

Before I was able to reach the bend in the trail which led back to the main road and home, Holly turned me around. Kobi was out of the bushes and back on the trail. Both he and Daisy were laughing.

"Really?" Daisy asked over her shoulder to Holly. "She trots to safety?"

Hey! I didn't know what was going to happen next. I felt I should conserve my energy until I needed it!

"As far as spooks go, she's pretty tame," Holly said as she squeezed my ribs to catch up with Daisy. "What was it?"

"It was a vulture on the ground." Daisy's hand trembled a little as she wiped the sweat from her face. "Kobi thought it was the Bird of Death coming for him. Thankfully the palmettos stopped our wild ride."

Kobi snorted.

"Let's just finish the loop and head on home."

I second that!

CHAPTER 9 – THE ACCIDENT

I hated winter. It had been cold and rainy for at least a week. Daisy left our blankets on us for a few days, so when the sun finally came out and our blankets came off, it gave us reason to celebrate.

Kobi and I tore across the pasture, slipping and sliding through the mud. He'd chase me for a while, then I'd turn around and chase him. I'd never seen him *really* play before. It was nice to see he could. And, I had to admit that I quite enjoyed moving at a fast speed for a change. At times even Cuzzin would get in on the fun. Since he hurt his hip again, he couldn't run as fast, but he still seemed to enjoy the chase, barking and carrying on like an idiot, always stopping short of actually catching one of us. I guess he had learned his lesson.

Daisy called us in for dinner, and I turned too fast. My legs shot out from under me and I slammed to the ground. Hard!

Kobi snickered as he trotted past. "Need to watch where you're going next time."

I staggered to my feet and shook it off. But when I put my front left leg on the ground, something didn't feel right. It wasn't a blinding pain, just a little tweak in my muscle.

I walked to the barn and then into my stall. *Maybe after I eat my leg will feel normal again.*

After dinner, I couldn't pick my hoof up high enough to clear the slight ledge on the outside of the barn. I tripped. Daisy gave me a funny look, as if she caught a whiff of something stinky. Instead of turning and leaving us outside for a few hours as she normally did, she watched me walk. I headed over to join Kobi at the hay pile, limping a little and favoring my front leg.

Daisy watched the entire time. Was she thinking about my limp or back to when her old horse Jake went lame?

Kobi wandered to the pond to drink. I only drank when he did. I figured that whatever squirmed beneath the surface would go after him first, and that would give me time to escape. Friend or not, I wasn't going to put myself in unnecessary danger, not if I could help it. My hooves sunk into the mud deeper than usual. I had to pick my legs up high to get them out. I tugged on my left leg. Pain shot all the way up to my shoulder.

This can't be good.

I got all my feet moving again, but anytime I put weight on my left foot my knee and shoulder hurt.

Kobi noticed the way I threw my leg forward. He came back and nudged my hindquarters. "Why are you doing that?"

"My leg hurts. I don't want to put any weight on it."

Kobi seemed to think it over for a minute. "Maybe you shouldn't walk on it then. Just graze right here."

"Here? Next to the pond? What if something tries to attack me? I'd never make it."

"What do you think is living in that pond? Not that it matters. You wouldn't be able to outrun anything anyway, limp or not. You are the slowest horse I've ever met."

"And you're the foolish horse who is silly enough to stand so close to trouble, trouble that might eat you." I squealed at him.

We heard Daisy clap, signaling it was time to go in to our stalls for the night.

Kobi chuckled. "Eat me? Really!" And off he trotted to the barn.

"Sugar! Come on, girl. Time for bed."

I took a step forward and almost collapsed from the pain. I'd never make it to the barn.

"Rex, I can't find Sugar. She's not coming in. Can you grab a flashlight and help me look?"

I whinnied. Rex scanned the pasture with sweeps of light.

"I'm over here!" I yelled when the beam of light came close.

Rex came to my side. I held my front leg out for him to see.

"I found her," Rex yelled. "But you need to get over here. She can't walk."

Daisy rounded the corner of the house with my halter slung over her arm.

Good. With both of them here, they should know what to do.

"What's taking so long?" Kobi mumbled, his mouth full of grain for our bedtime snack.

We ignored him as Daisy slid my halter over my nose and tugged gently. "Come on, Sugar. We need to get you to the barn so I can see what's wrong."

I leapt forward, trying to keep as much of my weight on the other three legs.

"Wow, this is bad," Daisy whispered.

But I could hear well enough. *How bad?*

Rex ran ahead to open the gates so we could take the shortcut to the barn through the grass of the Forbidden Zone. I limped along as best I could. Daisy would make me walk five or six steps before letting me take a break. It felt like the longest walk ever. When we went through the backyard, I was so busy trying not to fall that I didn't even try to graze. The light in the barn was pulling me in. Safety in my stall.

As soon as we were close enough for the water hose to reach, Daisy flipped the lead rope over my neck and rinsed my legs off. The cold water was a shock since the night was chilly, but strangely it made my leg feel a little better.

After all the mud was washed away, Daisy led me, hopping, into the barn. Standing on the hard ground in the breezeway, Daisy handed Rex my rope and grabbed the hoof-pick.

Under normal circumstances, I didn't like to have my hooves picked since it meant balancing on three legs, but I knew I didn't have much of a choice that night. Daisy grabbed my hoof and pulled it to her to have a better look. She picked it out and tapped along the bottom and the sides of my hoof. She must not have seen anything and since I didn't flinch, she set my hoof down.

"Hmm, nothing there. Do you think she pulled a muscle?"

"Maybe. She was chasing Kobi earlier. She could have tripped."

I did! I did! That's exactly what happened! Except Kobi was chasing me and it started right before dinner. It's gotten worse since then. Please make the pain stop!

Daisy made some worried faces, then disappeared into the feed room. I hoped she was getting some cookies. *I could do with one or two about now.*

She came back, carrying a bottle of something. She pulled on a pair of rubber gloves before she opened the bottle and squirted some green goo onto her hand. It smelled minty. She rubbed her hands together then rubbed the goo down my leg.

My legs instantly tingled. It wasn't an unpleasant feeling, but I would have preferred cookies. Daisy's hands worked up and down my leg.

"I don't feel any cuts or swelling. None of her muscles are hot either." Daisy stood up.

"What about her chest and shoulder? Do you think she could have pulled that?"

"Maybe." Daisy rubbed some more of the green goo over my chest and shoulder. My front leg jumped when she prodded my shoulder.

"I think you found the spot."

Yes. Yes. That's the spot.

Daisy took her gloves off. "I think we've done all we can for tonight. I'll give her something for the pain and see if that and the liniment helps. If not, someone's on stall rest for a few days."

Someone? Stall rest? What's that?

Kobi stuck his nose over his wall. "Sorry to hear that. Stall rest stinks."

I wanted Kobi to explain what stall rest was, but Rex tugged on my halter to lead me into my stall. I hesitated a second until Daisy walked in with a bucket of feed. I limped in behind her.

*****

Kobi was right. Stall rest was awful. I was forced to stay in my room while Kobi wandered wherever he wanted. Anytime I lost sight of him, I would yell. If I had to stay in one spot, so should he.

Daisy must have thought I missed him, so she let him graze in the backyard, in the Forbidden Zone. I disliked him greatly for that. Here I was stuck in my stall and Kobi got to eat the sweet grass. That was for special occasions. What was more special than me being injured? *I should be out there, too.*

Daisy visited several times a day to rub that goo all over me. She not only tended my leg, but my neck, down my back, and all four legs. My skin twitched and tingled.

Ruth came out to see me and brought treats, but wouldn't take me from my stall. I'd have been happy bowing for her or even learning another trick. Ruth did kiss my cheek though.

I heard Daisy on the phone. "I need to schedule a farm visit. My horse is lame. Yes, please. I'd love an appointment today." She wandered over and scratched my ear. "I think we need professional help, girl."

Kobi stepped up behind. "The last time Daisy had a vet come out here for a lame horse, it was Jake. I never saw him again after that visit."

I couldn't tell if Kobi was just trying to be a jerk and mess with my head, or if he really was concerned. He never joked when it came to his old friend Jake.

This must be serious.

CHAPTER 10 – BOREDOM, AGAIN

Ruth combed out my mane as Daisy delivered the vet's news. Kobi had been turned out to graze, but stayed close by. He was as eager as I to hear the news.

"Somehow she got a fissure crack along the back of her knee. The x-rays didn't reveal any bone chips, which is good. The only cure for those are surgery."

I swallowed. *Surgery?*

I looked at Kobi. He just shook his head and returned to grazing.

"What do we have to do to heal the fissure crack?" Ruth put away the comb and grabbed a soft brush.

"The only thing we can do is put her on stall rest for thirty days," Daisy answered.

Stall rest? For thirty days? No!

"Did he say if she'll ever be able to be ridden again?" Ruth asked. "Or is she always going to be lame?"

Ooh, good question.

"He expects her make a full recovery. I still don't think we'll ever take her in any speed or timed events, but she should be fine for trail riding." Daisy reached over and scratched Kobi's ear.

"It's a good thing Rex is home most of the time. He can make sure she has hay and turn her out about a half-hour a day for exercise and a little sun." Daisy sighed. "It's going to be a long month."

*****

She wasn't kidding. It was the longest thirty days of my entire life. Thankfully Daisy put medicine in my food so she would be sure I'd eat it. It tasted like oranges and kept the pain at bay. I wouldn't normally eat an orange, but that orange-flavored stuff was okay. So, my leg didn't bother me and I could walk, if a little slower than usual. What bothered me the most was being alone. Anytime Kobi was out of my sight, I paced the stall and whinnied for him. Sometimes he would answer and let me know where he was, but most of the time he didn't. Jerk!

Rex allowed me to graze in the Forbidden Zone a couple hours a day so I could see Kobi. Kobi didn't like that. We were separated by fences, and he threw a couple of jealous comments my way. I didn't respond. I just kept eating. I was able to stretch my legs without having to worry about walking too far from my stall. The less I limped around, the longer Rex let me stay out. I didn't think Daisy had any idea how long I roamed around the backyard each day. Ruth came out every few days to groom and bathe me. But all in all, it was still very boring.

Long after my leg stopped hurting, I was again turned out during the days with Kobi. Things were a little better, but it occurred to me that I was still bored. I wandered over to where I could face him. His back leg was cocked and his bottom lip hung down, a sure indication he was sleeping. Daisy had worked him hard that afternoon. He was tired, but I didn't care. I needed to talk.

"Kobi? Are you awake?" I knew full well he wasn't.

He shifted his weight. "What do you want?" He spoke slowly as if still sleeping.

"I'm bored."

"Then go to sleep." He worked his jaw a little before settling back into a comfortable stance.

"No, that's not what I mean. I'm talking in general. Nobody does anything with me anymore. Daisy works you all the time and I'm left behind again. Even Ruth and Holly have quit coming out to see me."

Kobi moaned and walked up to his stall gate. He was awake. "It's summertime. Rex won't ride when the weather gets too warm. I think Ruth has to go to work during the day, so that just leaves Daisy. You know she only has enough time in the morning to spend with one of us before we get sweaty." He swatted at a horse fly. "And it's always going to be me. It's just the way it is."

"Well, what about Holly or even little Clementine? They used to visit when it got warm. I haven't seen them since I hurt my leg."

"Daisy's probably afraid you'll get hurt again if you're ridden. You know how she worries." Kobi backed away, letting me know the conversation was coming to a close. "Take a nap."

"Not yet. What can I do to make them give me a job? I hate just hanging around and watching you do all the fun stuff."

Kobi swished his tail again. I couldn't tell if the bugs were bothering him or if it was me.

"Most horses would love to be a pasture ornament. Enjoy it while it lasts. They'll ride you again soon enough. Now let me get back to sleep."

"But I don't want to be a pasture ornament. I want a job. I need a job."

Kobi didn't respond. The sound of his steady breathing told me he had returned to his nap.

CHAPTER 11 – ESCAPE

A few weeks later Holly let us out of our stalls in the morning.

"Have you seen Daisy or Rex lately?" asked Kobi.

I tried to think back to when I last saw them. "It's been a while."

"Even Cuzzin hasn't been around."

"Do you think something happened to them?"

Kobi's eyes widened for a split second. "I hope not. Nobody is going to spoil me like Daisy does." He looked over at the front gate, the same gate Rosemary drove through all those months ago when I arrived.

"You're right about that," I agreed.

He pinned his ears at the comment and snapped his teeth together. I backed up a few steps. He looked back at the gate. "Should we go look for them?"

The metal gate was shut. It was only open when someone drove through.

"How would we get out?" I didn't know how to manipulate a clasp. "And if we did, where would we look?"

"I don't know." It sounded as if he were about to start whining. "What if they're in trouble?" He ran to the front field.

I stayed in the back until a breeze kicked up. A snap sounded from a tree. I didn't like it. I trotted away, stood beside Kobi and dropped my head to graze. The tree limb snapped and fell to the ground. I was glad I moved.

"Hey, Sugar. Look!"

The front gate swung open in the wind, and no one was around to drive through or close it.

"You've been complaining about being bored. Here's our chance for an adventure. And to find Daisy."

I wasn't too sure about the idea Kobi was pushing. Yes, I'd been bored. Yes, I wanted an adventure. But how safe would I be on the other side of the fence without our humans knowing where we were? I shouldn't have mentioned Daisy was missing. Kobi's idea to look for her seemed foolish. Before I could tell him what I thought, his dark rump passed through the gate and his hooves clomped along the road.

Mine soon clomped alongside his. "Now what do we do?"

He looked down the street. "We should head that way. Their cars come from this way when they drive home."

Kobi's plan sounded somewhat logical, and I followed him down the paved road. When we got to the end, we had another choice: left to where Daisy and Holly would take us out to trail ride, or right into the unknown. Both directions looked about the same, black road as far as our eyes could see, green pine trees and long grass running along both sides of the road.

"Now what do we do?"

A car zoomed past. The horn blared and petered off in the distance.

"We could follow them and see if they take us to Daisy and Rex," Kobi suggested.

That plan didn't make any sense. We'd never keep up with the car. I wouldn't anyway.

"Let's eat a little first," I said. "I'm getting hungry. Besides we've never tried the grass this far away. It may be the best we've ever had."

Kobi swished his tail, but didn't argue. He wandered a little to the right, the opposite direction to the way we ride with Daisy and Holly, then dropped his head and grazed.

The long grass tasted the same out here as the short grass did at home. I was disappointed. I was hoping for something sweet, something still covered by the morning dew.

A log truck zoomed by, rattling its chains and metal parts. I expected Kobi to spook, but he didn't pay it any attention.

And then another truck.

And then another car.

I didn't like their noise or their speed. It all worried me. I saw a yard with grass, away from the road. The gate was open. I swished my black tail to get Kobi's attention. He followed.

We were only in the yard a few minutes when a man appeared from the house. He seemed familiar. Who was he? I couldn't conjure a memory. He moved slowly toward the gate. He was going to lock us in!

A dog barked. The sound came from inside the house. The bark was familiar, too, but I didn't want to hang around. I didn't want to be locked in, and I certainly didn't want to have a boxing match with a dog.

"Run!" I yelled. I'd rather take my chances on the open road with the opportunity of finding Daisy and Rex. I didn't want to be trapped in somebody's yard that I couldn't recall. "Run!" I called again.

Kobi followed through the open gate.

"Kobi! Sugar!" he yelled.

The man knew our names. I wasn't going to stop and ask why. I feared for my life. I bumped Kobi out of the way and led our escape down the road, moving in the same direction we were going before stopping at that yard. As I ran vibrations shot up my leg, making the back of my knee hurt again. I kept going, leading us away from that man who wanted to catch us. Our hooves hit the hollow sound of a bridge, and we kept going. Kobi stayed with me the entire time. When I started to pant, I decided we had to be far enough away and we slowed to a walk.

"That was close. If he captured us we may never find Daisy. Hey, Sugar, you had a bit of speed up there."

"I was scared. But didn't you think it was strange he knew our names?" I asked, still a little out of breath.

"He did? I didn't hear what he was yelling."

"He looked familiar, too. I just don't remember where I've seen him."

Kobi looked back. Those eyes were deciding whether to return and investigate.

"What do we do now?"

He shook his head. "Do you not have a brain of your own? That's the third time you've asked me that."

"But …"

He kept on with the direction we were heading. We found another patch of long grass, almost to our knees. It was the kind that had the 'V' shape on the top and the small black spots that always got caught in my nostrils and made me sneeze. But Kobi decided to get off the road again and graze, so I followed.

A truck pulled up. I didn't like what was happening.

"What do we …" I didn't finish the question.

We trotted into a yard beside the patch of long grass. The truck followed. I *really* didn't like what was happening. The familiar man we had just run from jumped from the truck. A woman was with him. She also looked familiar. And then a third human. It was Daisy's dad. He carried our halters with him. I could see my pink halter. There was a dog tied in the back of the truck. It barked.

Cuzzin? What was Cuzzin doing with those people?

The man took Kobi's halter and the woman took mine and approached us carrying apples. It suddenly popped into my head where I knew them from. They always brought us juicy, red apples, and fed us over the top of the fence at home. These were safe people. They just wanted to bring us back home.

I looked at Kobi. Was he was ready to quit the adventure? He dropped his nose into his halter, and then tried to drag the human down the road with him, still not wanting to stop the search.

I also allowed the halter to be slid over my ears. It surprised me how much safer I felt with my halter on, and someone had my lead rope. We were going to be fine. We weren't going to find Daisy and Rex today, but maybe they would come home soon.

Home! I was never so happy to see our fence and pasture as I was that day. I was even happy to see Cuzzin. The human I was with walked me right through the gate. I didn't give them any trouble. Kobi, on the other hand, balked and had to be forced back inside the fence.

He yelled, "Daisy! Where are you?"

They managed to get Kobi inside the fence and closed the gate behind us before they took off our halters. Kobi ran around the pasture, pitching a fit. He was in a panic trying to find Daisy. I'd never seen him behave in that fashion. Again, I never should have mentioned she was missing.

Daisy's dad walked up to us. "Wait until they find out about this. They'll never take another vacation again."

I knew what vacation meant. And I knew who *they* were. Daisy and Rex had gone away for a holiday. These people were looking after Cuzzin. Daisy and Rex would be home soon. All humans came home from vacation. We were now safe and sound at home and Daisy and Rex would be home soon.

Cuzzin barked and barked. He was a brave old thing … from a distance.

CHAPTER 12 – NEW BEGINNINGS

A few days after Daisy and Rex returned from their vacation, we fell into our same summertime routine. Breakfast, hay, watch Kobi be groomed and worked, turned out in the pasture, treats from people over the fence, graze some more, in for dinner, turned out again and then back into our stalls for bedtime. There wasn't much of a change. Boring!

The same thought gnawed at the back of my mind over and again. *I need a job.* There had to be more to life than being a pasture pet. Kobi was ridden almost every day so at least his body and mind stayed active.

What about me?

One steamy afternoon, Daisy brought us into our stalls early. I didn't complain. I could stand in front of my fan and cool down somewhat. Sweat ran down places that sweat just shouldn't be. While I was enjoying my fan and snacking in my stall, a woman in a black bikini top, shorts, and boots arrived.

The woman asked Daisy if she could take me out of my stall.

A new rider? She was nowhere near as big as Vickie. She was smaller than Ruth and Daisy. But not as small as Clementine. She had two hands, unlike Rex. Daisy grabbed my halter from the hook and handed it to the stranger. She seemed competent as she slipped the halter over my nose and ears and led me from my stall.

This is looking good.

Daisy then proceeded to list all that she perceived was wrong with me, from my lazy side and my sticky stifle, to my recently recovered knee injury.

I couldn't believe her. How would she like it if I told some new horse, who hadn't met her before, all of her issues? How about her need to teach us not to be afraid of things by repeating the situation over and over? Or how she can't slow down to take a breath or allow us a moment to catch ours when she works with us? Or how Kobi is always picked first for treats?

The woman ran her hands over my four legs then braced her hands on my back as if she was going to jump right on and ride me bareback.

"Don't worry, girl," she said, taking a step back.

I'm not worried. And I'm not lazy. I just don't like running. And I don't have a sticky stifle, I just—

"It's too hot. I'm not going to hop on."

You're not? Okay!

I like how she talked to me. Her voice was calm and pleasant. She smelled like hay, grass, and something else sweet and edible. Her blonde hair hung down in waves from her cowboy hat. She listened to Daisy, ignored Kobi, and talked to me. I was so caught up with being the center of attention that I only caught the tail end of what Daisy said.

"So I think she'd be perfect for equine therapy."

Equine therapy? Equine therapy? What's that? Is it fun? It sounds fun. It probably is fun. As long as I have something to do, it doesn't really matter. Yes, I want to do equine therapy! I'd be perfect for it!

"Okay," the new lady said. "I'll think about it and let you know in a couple of days. She's beautiful."

I am? I mean, yes, I am.

"And the kids would love her. I've just got to see if I can swing getting another horse."

Oh, more horses, too? That would be great. I hate it when Kobi rides off and leaves me alone.

She led me back into my stall and slid the halter off.

"Did you hear that Kobi? I may have a new job doing equine therapy!"

"Whatever that is," he grumbled and moved to stand closer to his fan.

*****

Days passed. I figured the lady with the kids and more horses and the equine therapy stuff didn't want me. I was disappointed, to say the least.

Then one day I thought Daisy had forgotten to turn us out of our stalls. I heard a truck rumble down the road with a horse trailer rattling behind.

Another horse? A new trailer? Is that for me?

The truck pulled up. It was the equine therapy lady. Daisy disappeared into the tack room and came out with my pink, rope halter, not the one I normally wore, but the one she used when working me from the ground.

The equine therapy lady was wearing her cowboy hat again. She took the halter from Daisy, tied it on, and led me out of the stall. We walked around the side of the house and I saw the open horse trailer.

It was for me!

She led me to the door and allowed me to stop and investigate. The floor looked solid and safe. It smelled like dozens and dozens of other horses.

Looks great!

She dropped my lead rope and I hopped right in.

I'm ready to go!

Daisy laughed. "I guess we didn't need to worry about how she was going to load."

The lady secured the bar at my rump and closed the door. "Thank you so much. I'm going to take great care of her."

"I know you will, Ardith."

Ardith. Her name is Ardith.

"That's why we did it. She's too good a horse to waste around here as a pasture ornament."

You got that right, Daisy.

The truck rumbled to life and pulled away. Kobi whinnied his goodbyes.

The trailer didn't seem to go too far before it stopped and the motor shut down. I inhaled deeply. There were a lot of horses close by, more than I could count.

Ardith unlatched the trailer's back gate and released the bar.

I wanted to make a good first impression for all the new horses I smelled. But how? *Don't slip would be a start.* I backed out and was careful on the step down. I lifted my head and saw several horses dotting the landscape, but not a fence anywhere. The closest horses looked just like me. White with patches of brown and black all over.

I whinnied before I surprised myself and actually galloped into the center of another herd.

Alrightly then, let's get the introductions started!

CHAPTER 13 – LIFE BEGINS AGAIN

I didn't see Ardith much the first few days, or many humans at all for that matter. But when she did come out, she would feed us grain and groom each of us in turn. That was our alone time with her – the grooming. She was really good at it and spent time on all my itchy spots. I never felt that it was a race to be clean or that she had other things on her mind, like I always felt with Daisy.

Since there were so many horses, I spent most of the first few days getting to know the rest of my herd. Or actually herds. We all lived together in one giant pasture, not separated by fences like in other places. It was nice. I had the opportunity to talk to everyone and decided who I wanted to spend time with. I liked the other paints the best and found myself going wherever they were. It was heaven. Acres and acres of grass, and turned out all day and night. I did miss that little mustang – just a little, but not enough to want to return to him and Daisy, and the same boring thing day after day.

The only thing I didn't like was that our water source was a large pond. The sheer size was quite intimidating. But the other horses drank from it without issue, so I did the same. But only when someone else was drinking first. If a horse-killing animal hid beneath the surface I didn't want to be first on the menu.

Ardith walked toward me carrying my pink rope halter one evening. "Alright, girl. Enough lounging about. It's time to get to work." She slipped the halter over my nose and tied it into place. "Let's see what you can do."

She led me to her truck and looped my lead rope around the hinge of the tail gate. Grabbing a soft brush, she stroked it across my coat in long, slow strokes.

Mmmm. I like this, Ardith.

I could have fallen asleep. She took time to investigate my legs, pick my hooves, and get all the tangles from my mane and tail. I was well behaved and didn't flick my tail a single time, even though I hated having to stand on three legs to get my hooves picked.

"There, now you look like a horse again."

What do you mean, again? What did I look like before?

Ardith tossed the pad on my back and slid it down my withers, getting all the hair to lie down right, before she heaved the saddle into place.

Ugh! I'd forgotten how heavy leather saddles were. Don't you have any like Daisy uses? They're much lighter. I like those better.

Ardith talked to me about her day as she tightened the girth, but never mentioned whether she had a lighter saddle. Oh, well.

As soon as I was tacked up, we stepped away from the truck. Ardith swung up into the saddle easily, as if I were a small pony, and she wiggled in the saddle to find the right spot. I didn't mind the movement. It wasn't as bad as Rex's wobbles, or Clementine's bouncing. She squeezed my sides.

As I took my first step, I discovered I no longer wished to fake my level of knowledge. If Ardith was going to give me a job as a therapy horse, I owed it to her to comply with her every command. And every time. Not every once in a while like I had done with Daisy, Rosemary, and everyone else in the long list of riders before them.

Ardith sunk down in her saddle, exhaling while she tightened the reins. "Whoa." I understood completely what that meant and stopped close to the gate of the round pen.

She swung from my back. "Alright, you know how to walk, stop and somewhat steer. Let's see what else you know."

She clipped a blue lunge line to my halter which was under my bridle and led me into the pen. Picking up the long whip, she sent me to the worn sandy path on the inside of the pen. "Get on," she said, pushing me out with the whip.

I walked around the pen a few times, keeping an ear on Ardith in the center but making sure I didn't get tangled up in the metal bars of the pen either.

"Trot," she commanded.

I ran all of the different speeds I knew associated with that word. I was much better with sounds like kissing and clicking and with leg commands. Humans sometimes didn't mean what they said.

"Trot," she said again, popping the whip behind my hindquarters, then she clicked to me.

Wait just a second. I need time to think first. I sped up until I was trotting around the pen in a choppy two-beat gait.

"Canter," Ardith said.

Hmm, canter? That can mean a couple of different things, too.

Ardith made the universal kissing sound for cantering and popped the whip behind me again.

Gotcha! I sped up again until I was moving around the pen in a three-beat gait, much smoother than my trot. My hip knocked the metal panel, but I kept my ear pointed toward Ardith.

What next?

She didn't give me another command for a while. She watched my legs as if they were the most interesting part of my body.

What's wrong? Am I limping or something? I feel fine. Her watchful eyes made me feel hot all of a sudden and I didn't want to canter anymore. I broke into a trot.

"No, I didn't ask for that. Canter." Ardith didn't wait for me to figure out her words. She made the kissing sound and popped the whip behind me again.

I sped up into a canter.

"Good girl."

She watched me go around the pen one more time. "Trot."

Again, words! I like sounds better.

She clicked and gently tugged the lunge line once. I slowed to a two-beat gait again.

"Walk."

I know that one. I immediately slowed.

"Good girl. Now whoa."

I am walking, or did you say whoa? Whoa and walk are similar words. What do you want?

Another tug on the lunge line. Ardith stepped in front of me.

What are you doing? I stopped so I wouldn't hurt her. *Are you crazy?*

"Good girl," she reached up and scratched my forehead. "We have a lot to work on."

I was afraid you'd say that.

"Ardith! Is that the new horse?" A girl ran to us, her brown curls bouncing with each step.

"It is. This is Sugar." She led me to the gate. "You're a little early for your lesson. Go get Calamity Jane from the pasture."

"Can't I ride *her* today?" the girl asked, pushing fly-away hair away from her eyes.

What? Ride me? I was just lunged!

"Oh, no. Sugar's not ready to be used for lessons yet. She still has a lot to learn."

Thank goodness. I'm tired.

"But she's so pretty." The girl had to reach up on her tip toes to scratch my neck. Her hand shook slightly, suggesting she wasn't as confident as her voice depicted her to be.

Pretty? Maybe I'm not so tired.

"No, she's not ready. And no more fussing, Callista. Go grab Calamity while I finish up. I'll meet you at the truck."

Ardith took off the lunge line and swung up into the saddle. "That's one little girl who won't take no for an answer. You two may be a good pair. You both just moved here and haven't made many friends yet." She squeezed my sides. "I love it when good ideas come to me."

CHAPTER 14 – THE BIRTHDAY PARTY

In the bustle of a late morning, Ardith caught Saltos — one of my pasture buddies —and me and took us to the front of the pasture for breakfast away from the rest of the herd. It was unusual for the two of us to be singled out. Ardith was alone, so we weren't going trail riding. And it wasn't a lesson, because her students collected those horses. It was strange, but I put those thoughts from my head and focused on my extra meal.

"Ardith? Are you out here?"

Daisy?

"Yeah, I'm over here."

Daisy walked past, patting my rump on her way.

Daisy! What are you doing here? I hope you didn't bring Kobi with you.

"Thank you for helping today," Ardith said. "Especially on such short notice."

Help? Help with what?

"I'm glad I can. Just tell me what you need me to do."

"I don't know how many of these kids have been around horses before, and I don't know about their vision. Some will have limited vision, and some, none. I figure we can split into two groups. I'll take Saltos and you can take Sugar."

Oh great, I'm stuck with Daisy.

"We'll start with the kids touching the horses. They can get to know them, ask questions, and stuff like that. Then we'll put them on bareback so they can feel the movements as we lead them around. The parents can walk beside and steady their child." Ardith handed Daisy some brushes. "Do you mind grooming Sugar?"

"Not at all."

I guess this is one of my big tests. Children with limited sight. They're going to rub me down, and then I'll take them around bareback. I hate bareback. But, after all, it's a job, and I wanted to work.

Daisy took the brush and started grooming me, paying close attention to the white spots.

Ah, you remembered how itchy I am there? Maybe it won't be too bad to be partnered with you after all, Daisy.

When they were done grooming us, they slid our halters up our nose and clipped on the lead ropes.

"We'll walk the horses down to the kids and then down to where I have piles of hay," Ardith took Saltos to the gate. "The horses haven't done birthday parties before, but I trust these two to just stand and eat while the kids touch."

I heard kids squealing from a line of cars before they even stopped. As soon as the doors opened, the kids feet hit the ground and they dashed toward us. Ardith stood in their path like a guard.

"Stop right here. I know you're all excited, but we have to go over some rules first."

Yes! Rules are good.

"First of all, no running. Second, no screaming or yelling. And the third rule is the most important of all. Are you ready?"

All of the children nodded their heads.

"You have to have fun!"

The kids laughed.

She split them into two groups, one for her and Saltos and the other for me and Daisy. I was surrounded by eight children and their parents.

"Sugar's a big girl," said Daisy. "But she's really gentle. I want you all to start with her front legs. Feel where they meet the ground."

Eight pairs of hands played with my hooves.

"The hard, hairless part is her hoof. Now slide your hands up, feel her legs and knees. As you move your hands higher, you'll feel her chest."

Small fingers massaged up my legs. I liked it. I closed my eyes and enjoyed the attention. I licked my lips, but when the fingers reached my chest they probed the little crease behind my legs. It tickled. I opened my eyes and snorted.

Daisy rubbed my forehead. "It's okay, girl."

I know it's okay. It just tickles.

"Now feel her muscular shoulders and the bottom of her belly. Rest your hands there a minute and feel her breathing. Inhale and exhale."

My stomach grumbled.

A girl giggled. "She must be hungry."

"Sugar's always hungry," Daisy explained. "Their stomachs are always rumbling and digesting their food. If their bellies are quiet, then we have a problem."

Plus, you know Daisy, I'm always hungry. I dropped my head to take a bite of the alfalfa hay Ardith gave us as a treat. *I would do anything to eat alfalfa more often. Get them to rub me again, Daisy, please.*

"Now, gently trace your hands down Sugar's back legs. Feel where her hock points out. And then down to where her hoof touches the ground."

It went on this way as the kids felt almost every inch of me with their fingers. Daisy pointed out my tail, my thin mane and fluffy forelock. For those that were brave enough to want to touch my head, Daisy pointed out my ears, nostrils, and the line of my jaw. For the really adventurous ones, Daisy showed them how to tickle my lips.

"Now, who's ready to ride?" Daisy asked.

I saw every hand shoot to the sky. *One at a time, right?*

"The birthday girl gets to go first."

Phew. I hated carrying more than one person at a time. They tended to move differently and have different balances. It always made me stumble a little.

"I'll need you to lift your child up," Daisy told the parents.

Zoe, the birthday girl, was the first child up.

"We'll stand here for just a minute and let you get the feel of Sugar underneath you," Daisy said. "Let me know when you're ready for her to walk."

Zoe wiggled around on my back a little, looking for a comfortable place. She wove her fingers through my mane at my withers. "I'm ready," she said. I couldn't tell if her tone was one of confidence or wracked with nerves.

Daisy held my halter strap at my nose and tugged me forward. "Walk up," she said.

Remembering what Daisy's cues were, I took a step forward. Zoe swayed a little, but her father held fast to her leg as he walked beside us.

"Look at me! I'm riding a horse." Zoe squeezed her legs against my side

When someone squeezes my sides, I have to trot. But I had a sneaking suspicion that it didn't mean that in this instance. Daisy kept a tight grip on my lead rope.

"Just walk, girl," she whispered.

Don't worry. That's all I want to do.

Daisy led child after child around on my back, at a walk, of course.

After they wiggled and squirmed on my back to find a comfortable spot, it wasn't bad. I felt loved and valued like I had never experienced before. The children were so honest with their emotions of excitement and genuine affection.

That was one of the best days of my life.

CHAPTER 15 – MY OWN JOB, MY OWN GIRL

I fell into a new routine. As soon as I saw Ardith's black truck pull onto the property, me and her other four horses, Saltos, Lefty, Hank, and Calamity Jane would meet her at the side pen for a snack. Ardith groomed us while we ate; always starting with me and moving on to Saltos. Sometimes she groomed one of the other horses, but since they were mainly used as lesson horses, she usually left the grooming to whoever was receiving the lesson. I liked when Callista visited the best. I wasn't up to giving her a lesson yet, but she groomed me nicely. I hated that she always seemed so nervous. She always tried hard and meant well. Ardith had others groom me sometimes, too. They all had more confidence around me than Callista, but didn't do nearly as good a job.

After snack and grooming, the other horses were released and I was tacked up for our daily session. Sometimes Ardith just lunged me, other times she lunged me before she rode. But she always lunged me.

I learned quickly that the word 'trot' and clicking meant the two-beat gait, whether Ardith was on my back or on the ground. I also learned the word 'canter' and kissing meant the faster three-beat gait. I struggled with the words 'walk' and 'whoa' while lunging, but understood her seat and leg commands when she rode. It was tricky, having had so many different people ride me in the past with their different expectations and their different commands. Rosemary and Daisy clicked and kissed, Vickie just kicked, and Rex used words. So confusing.

I hope I get the hang of it soon. I slowed from a trot when Ardith sank down in the saddle and said, "Walk."

"That's it!" Ardith almost yelled at me. I jumped. She was always so calm. This time her voice was so different. She scratched my neck on the white spot. I liked her touch.

"Let's try it again." She squeezed and clicked. "Trot."

I moved quicker into the two-beat gait.

She exhaled and sat deep in the saddle. "Walk," she said, and tightened the reins.

I slowed down.

Ardith scratched my neck again. "That's what you needed. Someone on your back to give you the commands *and* the words. Not from the ground. I knew you'd get it."

A small, blue car appeared from around the corner. "Callista's here, so we'll have to stop for the day, or ..." Ardith finished her sentence on a high note. She was planning something.

Ardith walked me to where Callista was waiting. "How would you like to help me with Sugar today?"

Callista's eyes lit up with a sparkle. "Really? I'd love to!"

"Great. We'll start with her on the lunge line just to be safe. We need to work on her walking and stopping and I need someone on top who knows what I want. You'll be perfect." Ardith slid to the ground.

Callista grabbed her helmet and Ardith gave her a leg up. She gathered up my reins once her feet were secure in the stirrups. Thankfully she was not a bouncer. When her butt hit the saddle she didn't move.

"You won't need those," Ardith said, taking the reins from her and running the lunge line through my bridle. "She seems to be able to trot or steer, but not both at the same time." She unclipped the reins from my bridle. "You can either hold onto the saddle horn, or work on your balance by holding your arms out to the side like we worked on last week."

"I think I'll hold on to start."

Good idea. I can't focus on keeping you balanced and listen to Ardith at the same time.

"I'll give you the verbal commands," Ardith said. "You give Sugar the leg and seat commands to match."

"Got it."

Got it.

I walked circle after circle, then trotted circle after circle. I stopped when I was told and moved back and forth from trot and a walk as was asked. That was more work than I'd done in weeks. My back leg was starting to droop a little where I had the stifle injury and I dragged my back toe a little in the sand.

"Can we canter?" Callista asked.

Oh, I don't know about that.

"I think we should end it here. You've both done amazing jobs today and remember we always want to end on a good note. We'll keep practicing and maybe in a couple of weeks you two can canter."

Thank you. I'm so tired I don't think I could canter a full circle right now.

*****

After that Ardith used me for a lesson every day for the next few weeks. We did the same thing. I lunged while she gave voice commands and the kids used their legs and seats to direct me. Some of the bigger kids had more confidence than Callista and worked on their balance by holding their arms out to the side. Some smaller kids possessed less confidence and barely squeezed me into a trot, or they'd scream when I lurched forward. The kids who worked on their balance flipped and flopped all over the place and I missed so many cues. And the screamers? Ugh! I had no use for them.

It was a relief when I heard Callista's car. I mean, the other kids were alright, and I liked having something to do, but I preferred her gentle voice and manners.

"Hi, Callista. Glad you're here," Ardith said.

Me, too.

"Grab Sugar's halter then start grooming. I need to talk to your parents."

"How are you today, girl?" Callista asked, brushing the tangles from my tail. "The weather's finally starting to get cooler. Maybe we won't sweat as much today."

That would be nice.

I moved my ear that was closest to Ardith to hear what she was saying. I could only catch every few words: "ready for the responsibility" and then a breeze picked up taking the words away from me and I missed what her parents said.

Finally the wind shifted back I heard "co-own" and my favorite word of all time, "feed."

What's going on?

Callista scratched one of my ticklish white spots. Ardith returned with two people.

"Callista, Ardith has an opportunity for you." That lady must be Callista's mom. "She's pleased with the hard work you've been doing and how often you come out to ride."

Callista stopped brushing and turned to look at the adults.

"Ardith wants to know if you'd be interested in sharing Sugar with her. You can come out and ride anytime you want, but you'll have some of the responsibilities, too."

Callista inhaled sharply and grinned. "Yes!" She threw her arms around my neck and buried her face in my mane.

Share? What does that mean for me? But whatever it is, it already feels fantastic.

"Okay," Ardith said. "What that means is you'll help me with her. She still has some training to go through. You'll also help me feed her and learn to take care of her."

I stopped listening after that. For me, it only meant one thing: I finally had a little girl of my own.

I'm so happy, I have found my forever home.

Thank you so much for reading Sugar's story, I hope you enjoyed it. Please let me know what you thought!

-Heather Hamel

Contact me at: heather.hamel@hotmail.com or through her website, www.HeatherHamel.com and don't forget to leave a review on Amazon and Good Reads!

Other books by Heather Hamel:

Horse Books:

Kobi: Memoirs of a Mustang
Sugar: My Journey Home
Saltos (Spring 2016 release)
Lefty (Spring 2016 release)

Ghostly Mysteries:

Murder of Crows
Destruction of Wild Cats (Fall 2016 release)

Cryptozoology Series

Within Emerald Forests (Book 1)
Under Sapphire Skies (Book 2)
Beneath Diamond Waters (Book 3) Fall 2016 release
Across Ruby Fields (Book 4) Winter 2016 release

Contact Heather at: heather.hamel@hotmail.com or through her website, www.HeatherHamel.com

www.ingramcontent.com/pod-product-compliance
Lightning Source LLC
LaVergne TN
LVHW042251121224
799027LV00006B/81